French Idioms and Expressions

C.W.E. Kirk-Greene

foulsham

LONDON • NEW YORK • TORONTO • SYDNEY

foulsham

The Publishing House, Bennetts Close, Cippenham, Slough,
Berks SL1 5AP, England.

By the same author: *Colloquial French*

ISBN: 0–572–02342–1

Typeset in Great Britain by Ann Buchan (Typesetters),
Shepperton, Middlesex.

Printed in Great Britain by St Edmundsbury Press Ltd,
Bury St Edmunds, Suffolk.

Contents

Preface

French idioms, like all idioms, add colour to speech and writing – as you will easily see from the quotations from various authors included in this book – and to have a grasp of them is essential for anyone wishing to take a step forward in fluency and comprehension.

Apart from being useful to know, idioms offer a fascinating study for those who simply enjoy language. Sometimes they seem to reflect clearly their nationality: for instance, *être de l'autre côté de la barricade* (page 16), *ouvrir un boulevard* (page 20), *mettre de l'eau dans son vin* (page 46). Comparisons of proverbs can surprise: *ne réveillez pas le chat qui dort* (page 29).

Some French idioms can be difficult and puzzling, but the expressions chosen for this book, whether fairly basic or more advanced, are relatively learner-friendly as their imagery is neither obscure nor complicated.

The book also includes an at-a-glance vocabulary of key words and as a further aid – or challenge – some revision tests. I hope it will offer an enjoyable way for students of French to expand their knowledge and usage of the language.

C. K-G.

Acknowledgements

I am very grateful to Mlle Audrey Setbon for so willingly making time to look through my typescript and for making several pertinent comments.

For reference, I am especially glad to have had at hand *Robert French Dictionary* (Collins,1987), *Dictionnaire des Expressions* (Bruno Lafleur, Bordas, 1984; Ottawa, Canada, 1979, Editions du Renouveau Pédagogique Inc.), *Dictionnaire des Expressions et Locutions Figurées* (Alain Rey et Sophie Chantreau), *Les Usuels du Robert*, 1979, as well as *A First Book of French Idioms* (C.W.E. Kirk-Greene, Basil Blackwell, 1973).

I would like to thank the publishers Jean-Claude Lattès, Paris, Presses de la Cité, Paris, Hachette Livre, Paris, and Mercure de France, Paris, for permission to use quotations from their publications.

I also wish to express my thanks to my editor and to my illustrator.

A

Abcès (M)

crever l'abcès   to grasp the nettle, to take the drastic action needed

crever	to burst

Accent (M)

mettre l'accent sur   to emphasise

*On a **mis l'accent sur** le fait qu'elle se trouvait au mauvais endroit au mauvais moment:* They stressed the fact that she was in the wrong place at the wrong time.

Affaire (F)

parler affaires   to talk business

c'est l'affaire de   it is a matter of

***C'est l'affaire d'un** petit moment, c'est tout:* It will only take a moment, that's all.

J'en fais mon affaire: I'll deal with it.

faire l'affaire   to suit, to be what is wanted, to fit the bill

*Ce chiffon **fera l'affaire**:* This rag will do nicely.

avoir affaire à   to deal with

avoir affaire à la justice   to have a brush with the law

Aile (F)

voler de ses propres ailes   to stand on one's own two feet, to be independent

*Maintenant c'est au tour d'Edouard de vouloir **voler de ses propres ailes**:* Now it is Edward's turn to want to stand on his own two feet.

aile	wing

Aimable

être aimable comme une porte de prison   to be very disagreeable, surly

Air (M)

avoir l'air   to appear

*Il **a l'air** heureux:* He looks happy.

en plein air   in the open air

en l'air   idle

*Ce ne sont pas des menaces **en l'air**:* They're not idle threats.

être libre comme l'air   to be as free as air

sauter en l'air (de joie)   to jump for joy

*' "Là-bas", dit-il, "c'est le maquis. Il paraît qu'ils sont nombreux, ils attaquent des camions et des trains." Je **sautai en l'air**. "Et si on y allait?" '* ' "The maquis's over there", he said. "It seems there are a lot of them, they are attacking lorries and trains." I jumped for joy. "And how about us going there?" ' (*Un Sac de Billes*, Joseph Joffo, Jean-Claude Lattès).

Aller

aller tout seul   to be plain sailing

*En principe cela **va tout seul**:* In theory it's plain sailing.

aller de soi   to be obvious, to stand to reason

*Il **va de soi** que tous ces prix vont bientôt augmenter:* It stands to reason that all these prices will soon go up.

Âme (F)

pas âme qui vive   not a living soul

*Il n'y avait **pas âme qui vive** dans la rue:* There wasn't a living soul in the street.

Il n'y pas âme qui vive dans la rue.

Amérique (F)

un oncle d'Amérique   a rich relation (from whom you hope to inherit)

*Toi, millionnaire un jour? Tu comptes sur **un oncle d'Amérique**?*: You a millionaire one day? You are counting on a rich relation to remember you?

An (M)

bon an, mal an   taking one year with another

Ange (M)

être aux anges   to be in seventh heaven, over the moon

avoir une patience d'ange   to have the patience of a saint

Angle (M)

arrondir les angles   to smooth things over

Annales (F)

rester dans les annales   to go down in history

*Un été plutôt froid qui ne **restera pas dans les annales***: a rather cold summer which won't go down in history

Antipodes (M)

être aux antipodes (de) — to be completely different (from)

*Il est toujours très bavard **aux antipodes de** son frère taciturne:* He is always very talkative, the dead opposite of his quiet brother.

Apôtre (M)

se faire l'apôtre de — to become the spokesman for

*Il **s'est fait l'apôtre de** la lutte des sans-toit:* He has become the spokesman for the struggle of the homeless.

apôtre	apostle

Apparence (F)

sauver les apparences — to keep up appearances

Arbre (M)

Les arbres cachent la forêt: You can't see the wood for the trees.

Argent (M)

en avoir pour son argent — to get one's money's worth

prendre pour argent comptant — to take as gospel truth

*Elle l'a lu et l'a **pris pour argent comptant**:* She read it and thought it must be true.

argent comptant	hard cash

Arme (F)

rendre les armes   to surrender, to give in

*Têtu, il refuse de **rendre les armes**:* He stubbornly refuses to give in.

faire ses premières armes   to start out, to make one's debut

*J'ai **fait mes premières armes** dans un hôtel au bord du Lac Léman:* I started off in a hotel on Lake Geneva.

(rester) l'arme au pied   (to be waiting) ready for action

*Les conservateurs attendent **l'arme au pied**:* The Conservatives are waiting, poised for action.

à armes égales   on equal terms

*Ce n'est guère une lutte **à armes égales**:* It's hardly an equal fight.

fourbir ses armes   to get ready for action

*Tous les partis politiques **fourbissent leurs armes**:* All the political parties are preparing for action.

fourbir	to furbish, to burnish

Arroser

*C'est **l'arroseur arrosé**:* it's (a case of) the biter bit

arroser	to sprinkle, to soak

Autorité (F)

faire acte d'autorité   to put one's foot down

Autre

nous/vous autres	
nous autres Anglais	we English
vous autres professeurs	you teachers
se sentir un autre homme	to feel a new man

Cela va beaucoup mieux, **je me sens un autre homme**: That's much better, I feel a new man!

Autruche (F)

faire l'autruche	to bury one's head in the sand

autruche	ostrich

Avenir (M)

L'avenir le dira: Time will tell, the future will show

Avis (M)

à mon avis	in my opinion
changer d'avis	to change one's mind

Avocat (M)

se faire l'avocat d'une cause   to defend, to champion a cause

se faire l'avocat de quelqu'un   to speak up for someone

avocat	lawyer

Avoir

Qu'avez-vous?   What's wrong?

Qu'est-ce qu'il y a?   What's the problem, what's up?

en avoir pour   to take

J'en ai pour deux minutes: I'll just be a couple of minutes.

B

Bain (M)

bain de foule walkabout (e.g. politician)

*Son **bain de foule** a continué malgré la neige qui tombait:* His walkabout continued despite the falling snow.

foule	crowd

Balle (F)

saisir la balle au bond to grab the opportunity, to jump at the chance

Il prend un bain de foule.

Barrière (F)

être de l'autre côté de la barrière/barricade — to be on the other side of the fence

*Maintenant que **je suis de l'autre côté de la barrière** tout le monde m'appelle 'Monsieur':* Now I'm on the other side of the fence everyone calls me 'Sir'.

Bâton (M)

mettre des bâtons dans les roues à quelqu'un — to put a spoke in it, to create difficulties for someone

Beau

être au beau fixe — to be set fair (weather)

*Sa vie professionnelle **est au beau fixe**, semble-t-il:* His professional life is going well, it seems.

être beau joueur — to be a good loser

avoir une belle peur — to have a nasty fright

les beaux jours — good weather

les beaux jours — heyday

les beaux jours du cinéma muet — the heyday of the silent movies

la belle saison — the summer months

*C'est **trop beau pour être vrai**:* It's too good to be true.

au beau milieu de — right in the middle of

*Ma belle-mère est entrée **au beau milieu de** son discours:* My mother-in-law came in slap in the middle of his speech.

de plus belle   all the more

*La grêle reprend **de plus belle**:* The hail comes on again even harder.

bel et bien   well and truly

*Cela a **bel et bien** compliqué l'affaire:* That has well and truly complicated the matter.

Beauté (F)

finir en beauté   to finish in style

*La neige est partout bonne et la saison va **finir en beauté**:* The snow is good everywhere and the season is going to finish in style.

Bec (M)

défendre bec et ongles   to defend vigorously, tooth and nail

*Il les **défend bec et ongles**:* He defends them fiercely.

bec	beak
ongle	claw

Besogne (F)

aller vite en besogne   to hurry things

*Il ne faut pas faire cela. C'est **aller trop vite en besogne!**:* You musn't do that. It's going about things too quickly!

besogne	work

Besoin (M)

si besoin est   if need be

Vous pouvez toujours me téléphoner avant huit heures **si besoin est***:*
You can always phone me before eight if need be.

Béton (M)

en béton   solid

des preuves en béton   rock-solid proof

béton	concrete

Bien (M)

**être du dernier bien avec
quelqu'un**   to be on the best of terms with
someone

Blason (M)

redorer son blason   to return to its former glory, its
former status

Il est très fier d'avoir **redoré le blason** *de cet hôtel:* He is very proud
to have restored this hotel to its former glory.

redorer	to re-gild
blason	coat of arms

Blessure (F)

panser ses blessures/plaies   to lick one's wounds

Le lendemain la ville **panse ses blessures***:* The next day the town is licking its wounds.

panser	to bandage

Bloc (M)

faire bloc   to unite

Toute la famille **fait bloc** *pendant cette crise pour le protéger:* The whole family is sticking together during this crisis to protect him.

Bois (M)

langue de bois   jargon, obscure (official) language

D'abord il faut comprendre leur **langue de bois***. Et ce n'est pas facile!:* First you have to understand their officialese. And it's not easy!

Bon

pour de bon   properly, really, seriously

Cette fois on va les examiner **pour de bon***:* This time they are going to be examined in earnest.

à quoi bon?   what's the point?

A **quoi bon** *écrire toutes ces lettres?:* What's the point of writing all these letters?

comme bon me semble   as I see fit

Je me couche **comme bon me semble***, souvent très tôt:* I go to bed as I see fit, often very early.

Bouche (F)

bouche à oreille word-of-mouth information

*Grâce au **bouche à oreille** il y avait une longue queue devant le magasin le lendemain matin:* Thanks to the word being passed around, there was a long queue in front of the shop the next morning.

Bouchée (F)

ne faire qu'une bouchée de to make short work of, to gobble up

*Quant à leur armée, il est sûr qu'il **n'en fera qu'une bouchée**:* As for their army, he is sure he will make short work of it.

bouchée	mouthful

Boule (F)

faire boule de neige to snowball

*C'est une chose insignifiante mais cela peut toujours **faire boule de neige**:* It's a trivial matter but it can always snowball.

Boulevard (M)

ouvrir un boulevard (à) to open the way, make it easy (for)

*Mais en faisant cela ils **ouvriront un boulevard** aux extrémistes:* But in doing that they will pave the way for the extremists.

Bourse (F)

sans bourse délier   without spending a penny

*Après le film vous pouvez poser des questions autour d'une tasse de thé, tout cela **sans bourse délier**:* After the film you can ask questions over a cup of tea, all without paying anything.

bourse	purse
délier	to undo

Bout (M)

joindre les deux bouts   to make ends meet

*Tout le monde semble dire la même chose – il devient de plus en plus difficile **de joindre les deux bouts**:* Everybody seems to be saying the same thing – it's getting harder and harder to make ends meet.

Brancard (M)

ruer dans les brancards   to be restive, rebellious

ruer	to kick out
brancard	shaft (cart)

Bras (M)

bras dessus bras dessous arm in arm

en bras de chemise in shirtsleeves

avoir le bras long to have a lot of influence

*Il m'a rappelé qu'il **avait le bras long**:* He reminded me that he had a lot of influence.

baisser les bras to give in

*La lutte continue; je ne vais pas **baisser les bras**:* The struggle goes on; I am not going to give in.

rester les bras croisés to stand idly by

*Il n'est pas du genre à **rester les bras croisés**:* He's not the sort to stand idly by.

avoir sur les bras to have on one's hands

*Et maintenant il a deux meurtres **sur les bras**:* And now he has two murders on his hands.

bras droit right-hand man

*Sur cette photo il parle à Georges, **son bras droit**:* In this photo he is talking to George, his right-hand man.

bras de fer trial of strength

*Le **bras de fer** entre eux ne fait que commencer:* The trial of strength between them is only just beginning.

baisser	to lower
bras de fer	arm wrestling

Bruit (M)

faire du bruit   to make a stir

*Son livre a **fait beaucoup de bruit**:* His book caused a big stir.

Le bruit court que . . .   the rumour is that . . .

Bureau (M)

On joue à bureaux fermés   it's a full house, sold out (theatre)

bureau de location	box office

Ils se promènent bras dessus bras dessous.

C

Carte (F)

mettre/jouer cartes sur table   to put one's cards on the table

brouiller les cartes   to muddle the issue, to confuse matters

*Il l'a fait exprès pour **brouiller les cartes**:* He did it on purpose to confuse matters.

connaître le dessous des cartes   to know what is going on behind the scenes, to be in the know

carte de visite   track record, background

*Il peut être fier de sa **carte de visite** – homme d'affaires, champion de tennis, pianiste:* He can be proud of his track record – businessman, tennis champion, pianist.

Cartouche (F)

brûler sa dernière cartouche   to fire one's last shot, to shoot one's bolt, to make a last attempt

cartouche	cartridge

Cascade (F)

en cascade   a spate of

des crises en cascade   one crisis after another

cascade	waterfall

Case (F)

le retour à la case départ   back to square one

*Oui, c'est **le retour à la case départ**. Nous allons reparler à tous les témoins:* Yes, it's back to square one. We're going to talk to all the witnesses again.

case	square (boardgame)

Cautère (M)

*C'est **un cautère** sur une jambe de bois:* It is an utterly useless remedy.

cautère	cautery, cauterising

Ceinture (F)

se serrer la ceinture   to tighten one's belt

*Eh bien, pas de vacances cette année! Je dois **me serrer la ceinture!**:* Well, no holiday this year! I must tighten my belt!

Cercle (M)

c'est la quadrature du cercle   to try to square the circle, to do the impossible

*Mais comment répondre à toutes ces lettres? Comment satisfaire tout le monde? **C'est la quadrature du cercle**:* But how to answer all these letters? How to satisfy everyone? It's trying to do the impossible.

Cerise (F)

la cerise sur le gâteau   the icing on the cake

*Qui plus est, **cerise sur le gâteau**, nous serons remboursés avant
Noël:* What's more, the icing on the cake, we'll be paid back before
Christmas.

cerise	cherry

Chacun

tout un chacun   anybody (at all), everybody (else)

*Après tout, **tout un chacun** peut écrire une letter au roi:* After all,
anyone at all can write a letter to the king.

Chair (F)

en chair et en os   in the flesh, in person

*Et puis un jour à l'aéroport je l'ai vu **en chair et en os!**:* And then one
day at the airport I actually saw him in person!

os	bone

Chaise (F)

se trouver entre deux chaises   to be between two stools, to be
                                    in a difficult position

Test Yourself!

PETITES REVISIONS 1
What is the missing word?

(Answers on page 128)

1. Il veut maintenant voler de ses propres - - - -. (to stand on one's own two feet)
2. Il est aimable comme une porte de - - - -. (to be surly and disagreeable)
3. Elle a une patience d' - - - - - -. (to have the patience of a saint)
4. Je vais essayer d'arrondir les - - - -. (to smooth things over)
5. Elle l'a pris pour - - - - comptant. (to take as gospel truth)
6. Il faut saisir la - - - au bond. (to grab the opportunity)
7. Maintenant je suis de l'autre côté de la - - - -. (to be on the other side of the fence)
8. Ils veulent nous mettre des - - - dans les roues. (to put a spoke in it)
9. C'est trop - - - pour être vrai. (to be too good to be true)
10. Je vais les défendre bec et - - - -. (to defend vigorously)
11. Le village - - - - ses plaies. (to lick one's wounds)
12. Je ne vais pas rester les bras - - - -. (to stand idly by)
13. C'est le retour à la - - - départ. (to go back to square one)
14. C'est un cautère sur une jambe de - - -. (to be an utterly useless step)
15. Elle l'a vu en chair et en - - -. (to see in the flesh)

Chance (F)

une chance sur deux   it's fifty-fifty, it's a fifty-fifty chance

'*"Tant pis, le risque a été pris, il n'y a plus à reculer. **Une chance sur deux**," pense Victor, qui s'efforce de maîtriser son émotion.*' ' "Too bad, the risk has been taken, there's no going back now. It's fifty-fifty," thinks Victor, who is trying hard to overcome his fright.' (Résistance Normande et Jour J, Raymond Ruffin, Presses de la Cité)

Chandelle (F)

brûler la chandelle par les deux bouts   to burn the candle at both ends

Chapitre (M)

*Sur ce **chapitre** on peut ajouter que c'est un pays très tolérant:* On that subject one can add that it is a very tolerant country.

chapitre	chapter

Charitablement

avertir quelqu'un charitablement   to give someone a friendly word of warning

Je l'avertis charitablement de ne plus jeter au panier les lettres que lui envoie le maire: I am giving him a friendly word of warning not to throw away the letters sent to him by the mayor any more.

Chat (M)

**ne réveillez pas le chat
qui dort**

let sleeping dogs lie

Château (M)

la vie de château

a luxurious life, the life of the
idle rich

**bâtir des châteaux en
Espagne**

to build castles in the air

Chaumière (F)

dans les chaumières

among simple folk

*Le message de notre vedette numéro un est bien simple – message qui
va faire pleurer **dans les chaumières**. 'Je divorce!':* The message of
our number one star is very simple – a message which is going to upset
ordinary people. 'I am getting a divorce!'

chaumière	thatched cottage

Ne réveillez pas le chat qui dort.

Chemin (M)

le droit chemin	the straight and narrow
la croisée des chemins	the parting of the ways
nos chemins se sont croisés	our paths crossed
faire du chemin	to make progress, to achieve something

*On a encore du **chemin à faire**:* We still have some way to go.

le chemin des écoliers	the long way round

*J'ai pris **le chemin des écoliers** pour arriver à leur maison:* I went the long way round to get to their house.

écolier	schoolboy

Cheval (M)

cheval de bataille	favourite theme

*L'enseignement a toujours été son **cheval de bataille**:* Education has always been his pet subject.

à cheval sur	astride, covering, straddling

*Une vie intéressante **à cheval sur** la Bourse et l'édition:* An interesting life covering both the Stock Exchange and publishing

Cheveu (M)

couper les cheveux en quatre	to split hairs

Cheville (F)

ne pas arriver à la cheville
de quelqu'un
not to be up to someone else's
standard

Merci pour tes félicitations mais je dois te dire que mon frère a publié une vingtaine de livres. ***Je ne lui arrive pas à la cheville:*** Thank you for your congratulations, but I must tell you my brother has published some 20 books. He's way above me.

cheville	ankle

Chien (M)

se regarder en chiens de
faïence
to stare stonily at each other, to
treat each other very warily

Un chien regarde bien un évêque: A cat may look at a king

faïence	earthenware
évêque	bishop

Chimère (F)

cela tient de la chimère   it's a bit of a pipe dream

Aujourd'hui ce plan ***tient de la chimère*** *– mais d'ici quelques années, qui sait?:* Today this plan is a bit of a pipe dream – but in a few years' time, who knows?

chimère	chimera, wild notion

Choix (M)

l'embarras du choix   a vast choice

Palaces, petits hôtels, appartements à louer. On a ***l'embarras du choix:*** Luxury hotels, small hotels, flats to rent. You're spoilt for choice.

Chorus (M)

faire chorus (avec)   to agree, to express agreement (with)

Mon oncle fait chorus avec mes parents: My uncle agrees with my parents.

Chose (F)

chose curieuse/étrange   strange to say

Chose étrange, ils ont refusé l'argent: Strangely enough, they refused to accept the money.

Ciel (M)

entrevoir un coin de ciel bleu   to glimpse a patch of blue sky

'Etes-vous plus optimiste maintenant?' 'Oui, j'entrevois enfin un coin de ciel bleu': 'Are you more optimistic now?' 'Yes, I can see a patch of blue sky at last.'

tomber du ciel   to arrive out of the blue, to come as a godsend

Et puis hier sa lettre avec son chèque sont tombés du ciel: Then yesterday his letter with his cheque arrived, out of the blue.

à ciel ouvert   open air

une patinoire à ciel ouvert   an open-air ice rink

Clair

en clair   in plain language

En clair les affaires marchent mal: To put it plainly, business is bad.

Classe (F)

faires ses classes   to do one's (basic) training

*J'ai **fait mes classes** chez un des meilleurs chefs de Londres:* I did my training with one of the best chefs in London.

Clin d'oeil (M)

en un clin d'oeil   in a flash, in the twinkling of an eye

***En un clin d'oeil** il fit disparaître le lapin:* In a flash he made the rabbit disappear.

clin d'oeil	wink

Cloche (F)

un autre son de cloche   a different point of view

*C'est **un autre son de cloche** chez les médecins:* You hear a different point of view from the doctors.

son	sound
cloche	bell

Clou (M)

enfoncer le clou   to hammer home the point

*Dans tous les couloirs il y avait des affiches pour **enfoncer le clou**:* In all the corridors there were posters to hammer home the point.

clou	nail

Coeur (M)

être de (tout) coeur avec quelqu'un   to feel for, to sympathise with someone

Je suis de tout coeur avec ces jeunes gens: I really do feel for these young people.

avoir quelque chose sur le coeur   to have something on one's mind

Je sais qu'il a beaucoup de choses sur le coeur: I know he has a lot on his mind.

ne pas porter quelqu'un dans son coeur   not to be very fond of someone

On dirait qu'ici on ne porte pas les pique-niqueurs dans le coeur: It seems they are not very fond of picnickers here.

si le coeur vous en dit   if you feel like it

Venez prendre un verre si le coeur vous en dit: Come and have a drink if you feel like it.

ce n'est pas de gaieté de coeur que   it is not with a light heart, it is unwillingly that. . .

Ce n'est pas de gaieté de coeur qu'on a décidé d'imposer ces sanctions, croyez-moi: We did not decide lightly to impose these sanctions, believe me.

à contre-coeur   reluctantly

Comble (M)

comble de malchance   a crowning misfortune

Comble de malchance, le garage venait de fermer: To cap it all, the garage had just closed.

comble	height

Complet (M)

au grand complet at full strength, in full

*Son équipe l'attendait **au grand complet** à la gare:* His whole team was waiting for him at the station.

Compte (M)

compte tenu de considering, taking into account

***Compte tenu de** tous ces problèmes, je vais attendre un peu:* Bearing in mind all these problems, I'm going to wait a bit.

au bout du compte/en fin de compte in the end, when all is said and done, all things considered

Conseil (M)

la nuit porte conseil it is best to sleep on it

conseil	advice

Copie (F)

copie conforme exact copy, replica

*Il a fait beaucoup pour la compagnie. Un homme exceptionnel. Et maintenant il prend sa retraite. Comment trouver sa **copie conforme**?:* He has done a lot for the company. An exceptional man. And now he's retiring. How are we going to find someone just like him?

Côté (M)

passer à côté de quelque chose   to miss out on something

*Lorsqu'on est jeune on a toujours peur de **passer à côté du bonheur***: When you're young you're always afraid of missing out on happiness.

Coude (M)

se serrer les coudes

to stick together, to show solidarity

coudes au corps

at the double

*'Maurice court déjà devant moi . . . "Attends! Je prends le vélo . . ." Il me fait signe que non et je le suis **coudes au corps**.'* 'Maurice is already running ahead of me . . . "Wait! I'll take the bike . . ." He signs to me not to do so and I follow him at the double.' (*Un Sac de Billes*, Joseph Joffo, Jean-Claude Lattès)

serrer	to grip
coude	elbow

Couleur (F)

annoncer la couleur

to declare one's hand, to announce one's intentions

*Dès son arrivée le nouveau directeur a **annoncé la couleur***: As soon as he arrived, the new headmaster made his intentions clear.

couleur	suit (of cards)

Coulisse (F)

en coulisse/dans la coulisse/ dans les coulisses	behind the scenes (often of politics)

*Mais qui sait ce qui se passe en ce moment **dans les coulisses?***: But who knows what is happening at the moment behind the scenes?

coulisse(s)	wing(s) (theatre)

Cour (F)

être bien en cour	to be in favour, to be well thought of

*'Malgré les réticences des services de comptabilité de la caserne (je n'étais décidément pas **bien en cour**), le colonel Bernard m'obtint la catégorie maximale.'* 'In spite of the reservations of the barracks' accounts department (I certainly wasn't in favour), Colonel Bernard got me the top category.' (*La Plastiqueuse à Bicyclette,* Jeanne Bohec, Mercure de France)

cour	court (royalty)

Courir

courir le monde	to roam the world
courir les supermarchés	to go round the supermarkets
un restaurant très couru	a very popular, fashionable restaurant

*L'assassin **court toujours***: The murderer is on the run, still on the loose.

Couronner

pour couronner le tout	to crown it all, to cap it all

Couteau (M)

être à couteaux tirés   to be at daggers drawn

*Depuis ce jour **je suis à couteaux tirés** avec mon ancien patron:*
Since that day I've been at daggers drawn with my former boss.

couteau	knife

Coûter

coûte que coûte   whatever it costs, whatever it takes

***Coûte que coûte,** je vais prouver que je suis innocent:* Whatever it costs, I'm going to prove that I'm innocent.

Coutume (F)

Une fois n'est pas coutume: Once in a while won't matter.

coutume	custom, habit

Couverture (F)

tirer la couverture à soi   to take all the credit for oneself, to take all the kudos

***Il tire la couverture à lui** en oubliant, bien sûr, combien ses collègues l'ont aidé:* He takes all the credit for himself forgetting, of course, how much his colleagues helped him.

couverture	blanket

Crabe (M)

un panier de crabes   they are always on at each other

Mais comment peux-tu travailler dans ce bureau? Il me semble que c'est **un panier de crabes**!: But how can you work in that office? It seems to me they are always on at each other!

Creux (M)

être au creux de la vague   to be in the depths of despair, really low

creux	hollow
vague	wave

Crible (M)

passer au crible   to examine closely

Tous les détails seront **passés au crible**: All the details will be closely looked at.

crible	sieve

Crier

crier à tue-tête   to shout at the top of one's voice

Il **criait à tue-tête** *et frappait à la porte*: He was shouting his head off and knocking on the door.

D

Date (F)

de longue/vieille date   long-standing

*C'est un ami **de longue date**:* He's a friend I've known for a long time.

Dé (M)

les dés sont jetés   the die is cast

*C'est trop tard pour tout nier. **Les dés sont jetés**:* It's too late to deny everything. The die is cast.

dé	dice

Dent (F)

en dents de scie   uneven, irregular

*Ces résultats **en dents de scie** ne lui ont pas plu:* These variable results did not please him.

scie	saw

Descendre

descendre dans la rue   to demonstrate (in the streets)

*Ce jour-là, vous verrez, beaucoup vont **descendre dans la rue**:* That day, you'll see, there will be a lot of people out demonstrating.

Désert (M)

prêcher dans le désert to be a lone voice speaking in vain

*L'Angleterre **ne prêche plus dans le désert**:* England is no longer a lone voice crying out.

prêcher ·	to preach

Désir (M)

prendre ses désirs pour des réalités to indulge in wishful thinking

Desserrer

ne pas desserrer les dents not to utter a word, not to open one's mouth

*'Durant le trajet de retour, **il ne desserra pas les dents.**'* 'During the return journey, he didn't open his mouth.' (*Les Années Américaines*, Pierre Galante, Annie Michel Gall, Jean-Claude Lattès)

desserrer	to unclench

Dessus

sens dessus dessous upside down, chaotic, topsy-turvy

*Ce matin le bureau est **sens dessus dessous**:* This morning the office is upside down.

Deux

à deux pas de   just a stone's throw from

*C'est un appartement calme mais **à deux pas des** grands magasins:*
It's a quiet flat but just a stone's throw from the stores.

à deux doigts de   within an inch of

*Elle était **à deux doigts de** révéler le secret:* She was within an inch of
giving away the secret.

*Ils sont **à deux doigts de** la faillite:* They're on the verge of bankruptcy.

pas	step

Diagonale (F)

lire en diagonale   to skim through, to glance at

*Quant à ta lettre, je n'ai eu que le temps de la **lire en diagonale**:* As
for your letter, I have only had time to glance at it.

Dieu (M)

à Dieu ne plaise!   God forbid!

si Dieu me prête vie   if God spares me

Il vaut mieux s'adresser à Dieu qu'à ses saints: It's best to go
right to the top.

ne pas être dans le secret   not to be privy or in the know,
des dieux   not to have been put in the
                                     picture by one's superiors

*Ah ça, je ne peux pas vous le dire. **Je ne suis pas dans le secret des
dieux**:* Ah, that I can't tell you. I am not privy to that.

jurer ses grands dieux   to swear to high heaven

Il a juré ses grands dieux qu'il n'avait jamais quitté la maison: He
swore to high heaven that he had never left the house.

Dire

c'est à dire	that is to say
cela va sans dire	that goes without saying
pour ainsi dire	so to speak
à ce qu'on dit	so it is said, reported

C'est un pays plus cher que le nôtre, à ce qu'on dit: It is a country which is more expensive than ours, so it is said.

on dit que	it is rumoured that
dire que	to think that

Dire qu'il aurait pu se casser la jambe: To think that he could have broken his leg.

aussitôt dit, aussitôt fait	no sooner said than done
c'est le moins qu'on puisse dire	to put it mildly

Elle n'en est pas très reconnaissante. C'est le moins qu'on puisse dire: She is not very grateful for it. That's putting it mildly.

autrement dit	in other words
et tout sera dit	and no more will be said

Elle n'a que s'excuser et tout sera dit: She has only to say she's sorry and that will be that.

c'est beaucoup dire	that's a bit strong

' "Je commence à être inquiet!" déclara Daniel. . . . "H'mm! . . . inquiet, **c'est beaucoup dire!**" protesta Arthur. "Il a pu avoir un simple accident, sans gravité!" ' ' "I'm beginning to be worried," Daniel declared. . . . "H'mm! . . . worried, that's going a bit far!" Arthur protested. "He could just have had an accident, nothing serious!" ' (*Michel et les Routiers*, Georges Bayard, Hachette Livre)

c'est peu dire	that's an understatement

Il ne l'aimait pas? C'est peu dire! Il la détestait!: He didn't like her? That's an understatement! He hated her!

qui dit . . . dit	as one . . . so the other

Qui dit voyages, dit tracasserie: Travel means hassle.

Dix

dix fois — time and again, several times, more than once

*On l'a menacé **dix fois** de renvoi:* He was threatened several times with dismissal.

Doigt (M)

compter sur les doigts de la main — to count on one hand

*De bons camarades comme ça, on les **compte sur les doigts de la main**:* You can count good friends like that on the fingers of one hand.

Dormir

ne plus en dormir — to lose sleep over it

*Je ne peux pas oublier tous ces problèmes, **je n'en dors plus**:* I can't forget all these problems, I'm losing sleep over them.

dormir comme un loir — to sleep like a log

dormir sur ses deux oreilles — to sleep easy, without worry

*L'argent est toujours là. Vous pouvez **dormir sur vos deux oreilles**:* The money is still there. You can sleep soundly.

loir	dormouse

Dos (M)

être/avoir le dos au mur
to have one's back to the wall, to be really up against it

se mettre quelqu'un à dos
to put someone's back up, to antagonise someone

*En agissant ainsi **il s'est mis tous ses collègues à dos**:* Acting in that way he has antagonised all his colleagues.

faire le dos rond
to adopt a low profile, to lie low (and let things pass)

Droit

marcher droit
to tow the line

*Mais si on travaille chez moi, il faut **marcher droit**. Tu comprends ce que je veux dire?:* But if you work here it means towing the line. Do you understand what I mean?

droit	straight

(dos) You scratch my back + I'll scratch yours
— Un petit service en vaut un autre

E

Eau (F)

se jeter à l'eau   to take the plunge

Je vais me jeter à l'eau et partir pour l'Australie avant Noël: I'm
going to take the plunge and leave for Australia before Christmas.

mettre de l'eau dans son vin   to water down one's claims, to
                                    climb down

'Leur réclamation est ridicule,' dit le ministre. 'Je leur conseille de
mettre de l'eau dans leur vin.': 'Their claim is ridiculous,' the minister
said. 'I advise them to be more moderate.'

il a coulé beaucoup d'eau   there has been a lot of water
sous les ponts   under the bridge

*Oui, depuis ce jour **beaucoup d'eau a coulé sous les ponts**, ma vie
a changé – en bien:* Yes, since that day a lot of water has flowed under the
bridge. My life has changed – for the better.

apporter de l'eau à son   to be grist to one's mill
moulin

*Franchement ce qu'il a écrit dans son autobiographie **apporte de
l'eau à mon moulin**:* Frankly, what he has written in his autobiography
is grist to my mill.

Egal

cela m'est égal   it's all the same to me, I don't
                                    mind

égal	equal

Eléphant (M)

*Il est **comme un éléphant dans un magasin de porcelaine**:* He's like a
bull in a china shop.

Test Yourself!

PETITES REVISIONS 2
What is the missing word?

(Answers on page 128)

1. Je me trouve entre deux - - - -. (to be between two stools)
2. Ne réveillez pas le - - - qui dort. (to let sleeping dogs lie)
3. J'ai pris le chemin des - - - - -. (to go the long way round)
4. Ne coupez pas les cheveux en - - - -. (to split hairs)
5. Elle a quelque chose sur le - - -. (to have something on one's mind)
6. La nuit porte - - - - -. (it's best to sleep on it)
7. Dès son arrivée il a annoncé la - - - -. (to make one's intentions clear)
8. Nous sommes à - - - - tirés. (to be at daggers drawn)
9. Une fois n'est pas - - - -. (once in a while won't matter)
10. Un ami de longue - - - - -. (long-standing)
11. J'habite à - - - - pas de la mer. (a stone's throw from)
12. A Dieu ne - - - -! (God forbid!)
13. Si Dieu me prête - - - -. (if God spares me)
14. Il vaut mieux s'adresser à Dieu qu'à ses - - - -. (it's best to go to the top)
15. Il est comme un - - - - dans un magasin de porcelaine. (to be like a bull in a china shop)

Enfant (M/F)

un jeu d'enfant child's play

*C'est **un jeu d'enfant** d'escalader le mur:* It's child's play to get over the wall.

bon enfant good-natured

une atmosphère bon enfant a relaxed atmosphere

*La police, **bon enfant**, ne faisait que regarder:* The police, in a good-natured mood, just watched.

Entendre

bien entendu of course

*C'est un petit village où, **bien entendu**, personne ne parle anglais:* It is a little village where, of course, no one speaks English.

(C'est) entendu I understand, right!

*Le petit déjeuner à huit heures? **Entendu**!:* Breakfast at eight? Right!

Envers

C'est le monde à l'envers: It's a mad, upside-down world.

Epée (F)

un coup d'épée dans l'eau an empty, pointless gesture

*Face à cette vague de cambriolages on décida d'organiser un colloque. Ce fut **un coup d'épée dans l'eau**:* Faced with this wave of burglaries, they decided to organise a seminar. It was a useless gesture.

épée	sword

Épine (F)

tirer une (belle) épine du pied to remove a problem for
à quelqu'un someone, to get someone out of
a nasty situation

Elle m'a tiré une belle épine du pied en payant toutes mes dettes:
She really helped me out of a nasty situation by paying all my debts.

épine	thorn

Esprit (M)

Les grands esprits se rencontrent: Great minds think alike.

Essai (M)

un coup d'essai a first shot, attempt

un galop d'essai a trial run

État (M)

un grand commis de l'Etat a high-up civil servant

une affaire d'état to-do

Remplacer mon passeport perdu est presque une affaire d'état:
Replacing my lost passport is a real to-do.

commis	clerk
état	state

Etoffe (F)

avoir l'étoffe de to have the makings of

*Certains disent **qu'il a l'étoffe d'un** champion de ski:* Some say he has what it takes to be a ski-ing champion.

étoffe	stuff, material

Etoile (F)

coucher à la belle étoile to sleep out in the open, under the stars

*Si je ne trouve pas de chambre **je coucherai à la belle étoile**. Pas de problème!:* If I can't get a room I'll sleep out in the open. No problem!

Il couche à la belle étoile.

F

Face (F)

faire face/voir les choses en face	to face it, to face up to things
sauver la face	to save face
perdre la face	to lose face

Facile

ce n'est pas chose facile de   it's no easy task to

Ce n'est pas chose facile de trouver un taxi après minuit: It's not an easy task to find a taxi after midnight.

Façon (F)

sans façon   simply, without fuss, without ceremony

Il m'a reçu sans façon: He entertained me informally.

'Voulez-vous du café?' 'Merci, sans façon.': 'Would you like some coffee?' 'No thanks, really.'

de toute façon   anyhow

De toute façon il aurait pu être beaucoup plus poli: Anyhow, he could have been much more polite.

Faim (F)

rester sur sa faim   to be left waiting for more

Dans votre dernière lettre vous avez parlé d'un scandale dans votre club. **Je reste sur ma faim**!: In your last letter you mentioned a scandal in your club. I'm waiting to hear more!

Faute (F)

faire/réaliser un sans-fautes   not to put a foot wrong

C'est un sujet délicat mais il a très bien parlé. **Il a fait un sans-fautes**: It's a tricky subject but he spoke very well. He didn't put a foot wrong.

Fendre

Il gèle à pierre fendre: It is freezing hard/cold.

fendre	to split, to crack

Fer (M)

une santé de fer   an iron constitution, very good health

croire dur comme fer   to have a firm belief, to believe strongly

Elle croit dur comme fer que la fin du monde est proche: It's her firm belief that the end of the world is nigh.

Feu (M)

jouer avec le feu   to play with fire

Avez-vous du feu?: Have you got a light?

*Il sort une cigarette et me demande **si j'ai du feu**:* He takes a cigarette and asks me for a light.

le feu vert   the green light, the go-ahead

*Dès qu'on recevra **le feu vert** je vous le dirai:* As soon as we get the go-ahead I'll let you know.

mettre le feu aux poudres   to set the cat among the pigeons

un feu de paille   a flash in the pan

faire feu/flèche de tout bois   to make use of all means available

les feux de l'actualité   the glare of publicity

*Il n'est pas toujours agréable d'être sous **les feux de l'actualité**:* It's not always pleasant to be in the full glare of publicity.

poudre(s)	gunpowder
paille	straw
flèche	arrow
feux	(spot)lights

Fil (M)

tenir à un fil   to hang by a thread

la paix tient à un fil   peace hangs by a thread

au fil de   with the passing of

au fil des mois   as the months go by

au fil des chapitres   as one goes through the chapters

donner un coup de fil à quelqu'un	to give someone a ring, to phone someone up

fil	wire

Finir

n'en plus finir — to go on and on

des discussions qui ***n'en finissent plus****:* endless discussions

Flèche (F)

monter en flèche — to shoot up

C'est comme toujours, soudain les prix ***montent en flèche****:* It's always the same, suddenly prices shoot up.

Flot (M)

à flots — in streams

Le soleil entre ***à grands flots****:* The sunlight streams in.

Le champagne coule ***à flots****:* The champagne flows.

flots	waves

Foi (F)

avoir la foi du charbonnier — to have a solid, simple faith

Il a 90 ans et il n'a jamais perdu ***la foi du charbonnier****:* He's 90 and has never lost his simple faith.

charbonnier	coalman

Fois (F)

une bonne fois pour toutes   once and for all

Je lui dirai, **une bonne fois pour toutes,** *que c'est impossible:* I shall tell him once and for all that it's impossible.

y regarder à deux fois   to think twice about it

'Vous avez été agressé?' 'Oui, et maintenant pour rentrer tard à pied **j'y regarde à deux fois**: 'You've been mugged?' 'Yes, and now I think twice about coming home on foot late at night.'

Fond (M)

de fond en comble   from top to bottom

La maison a été fouilleé **de fond en comble**: The house was searched from top to bottom.

Force

à force de   by dint of

Il a terminé son livre en six mois **à force de** *travailler sept jours sur sept:* He finished his book in six months by dint of working seven days a week.

Fortune (F)

faire contre mauvaise fortune bon coeur   to put a brave face on things, to make the best of a bad job, to grin and bear it

Foudre (F)

le coup de foudre   love at first sight

Elle n'hésita pas à acheter cette petite maison qui dominait la baie. Ce fut le coup de foudre!: She didn't hesitate in buying this little house overlooking the bay. It was love at first sight!

foudre	lightning, thunderbolt

Four (M)

Je ne peux pas être au four et au moulin   I can't be in two places at once

four	oven
moulin	mill

Frais

être frais comme un gardon   to be as fresh as a daisy

gardon	roach

Frais (M)

faire les frais (de quelque chose)   to bear the brunt (of something)

C'est les petits commerçants qui vont faire les frais de cette politique: It is the small shopkeepers who are going to bear the brunt of this policy.

frais	expenses, costs

Froid

garder la tête froide	to keep a cool head

Froid (M)

être en froid avec quelqu'un   to be on bad terms with
someone

Je suis en froid avec mon voisin de palier: I'm on bad terms with
my neighbour across the landing.

cela me fait/donne froid   that sends shivers down my
dans le dos   spine

Fusil (M)

changer son fusil d'épaule   to change tack, to change one's
ideas

Non, je n'écris plus. C'est fini, les romans. **J'ai changé mon fusil
d'épaule.** *Maintenant c'est la peinture qui meuble mes loisirs:* No, I
don't write any more. I've finished with novels. I've changed tack. Now it's
painting which fills my spare time.

fusil	rifle, gun
épaule	shoulder

G

Gâchette (F)

avoir la gâchette facile   to be trigger-happy

Gamme (F)

haut de gamme   up-market, top of the range

des hôtels de haut de gamme   top hotels

bas de gamme   down-market, bottom of the range

gamme	scale (music), gamut

Gant (M)

relever le gant   to accept the challenge, to pick up the gauntlet

*C'est à lui de **relever le gant**:* It is up to him to accept the challenge.

aller comme un gant   to suit perfectly, to a tee

*Je travaille à temps partiel ce qui me **va comme un gant**:* I work part time, which suits me down to the ground.

gant	glove

Gare

sans crier gare

without a word of warning, without any warning, out of the blue

'*Mais le surlendemain, dans la soirée, la veille de mon départ, une cousine de Paris arriva **sans crier gare**.*' 'But two days later, in the evening, on the eve of my departure, a cousin from Paris arrived without a word of warning.' (*La Plastiqueuse à Bicyclette*, Jeanne Bohec, Mercure de France)

Glace (F)

rompre la glace

to break the ice

*Elle a fait des plaisanteries pour **rompre la glace**:* She made some jokes to break the ice.

rester de glace/marbre

to remain unmoved

*Je lui ai tout raconté. J'ai presque pleuré, mais il est **resté de glace**:* I told him everything. I almost wept, but he remained unmoved.

marbre	marble

Grand

la grande vie

the good life, the high life

voir grand

to see things on a grand scale, to have big ideas

marcher à grands pas

to stride along

approcher à grands pas

to approach rapidly

*Noël **approche à grands pas**:* Christmas will soon be upon us.

grand ouvert

wide open

une fenêtre grande ouverte

a wide-open window

les grands absents   notable absentees

Parmi les grands absents hier soir le duc et son neveu: Among the notable absentees last night were the duke and his nephew.

les grands malades/blessés   the seriously ill/wounded

le grand public   the general public

au grand air   in the open air

une demi-heure d'exercice   half an hour's exercise in the
au grand air   open air

les grandes chaleurs   really hot weather

Venez passer quelques jours ici avant les grandes chaleurs: Come and spend a few days here before the weather gets really hot.

au grand soleil   in the bright sunshine

'Nos volets ont été tirés et dehors c'est encore le grand soleil.' 'Our shutters have been drawn and outside it is still bright sunshine.' (*Un Sac de Billes*, Joseph Joffo, Jean-Claude Lattès)

Il marche à grands pas.

Guerre (F)

à la guerre comme à la guerre

you must take the rough with the smooth, you can't pick and choose

c'est de bonne guerre

it's fair enough

Elle est allée travailler chez un autre éditeur. Cela arrive. **C'est de bonne guerre:** She went to work with another publisher. These things happen. It's fair enough.

de guerre lasse

weary (of the struggle)

Enfin **de guerre lasse,** *j'ai dit oui et j'ai signé:* Finally, weary with it all, I said yes and signed.

guerre	war
las	weary

Guichet (M)

jouer à guichets fermés

to play to a full house

guichet	box office

H

Hache (F)

enterrer la hache de guerre   to bury the hatchet

*C'est une mauvaise querelle. Ils devraient **enterrer la hache de
guerre**:* It's a pointless quarrel. They should bury the hatchet.

Hacher

**se faire hacher pour
quelqu'un**

to do anything for someone, to
be ready to die for someone

hacher	to mince, to chop up

Haie (F)

faire la haie   to line up

*Des marins **font la haie**. On attend l'arrivée de la princesse d'un
moment à l'autre:* Sailors line up. The princess is due at any moment.

haie	hedge

Haleine (F)

de longue haleine   long (and demanding)

*J'écris quelques pages chaque jour mais c'est un travail **de longue
haleine**:* I write a few pages every day, but it's a long job.

haleine	breath

Hâte (F)

n'avoir qu'une hâte just to want, to have only one desire

*Elle **n'a qu'une hâte**: revoir ses enfants en Angleterre:* All she wants to do is to see her children again in England.

hâte	haste

Haut (M)

des hauts et des bas ups and downs

*Comme tout le monde j'ai eu **des hauts et des bas** dans ma vie:* Like everyone else I've had my ups and downs in life.

Heure (F)

attendre son heure to bide one's time

l'heure H zero hour

vingt-quatre heures sur vingt-quatre round the clock

*Il y a une permanence **vingt-quatre heures sur vingt-quatre**:* There's somebody on duty round the clock.

Hier

cela ne date pas d'hier it's not new, it goes back a long way

*Vouz savez aussi bien que moi que c'est un problème **qui ne date pas d'hier**:* You know as well as I do that it's an age-old problem.

Hirondelle (F)

Une hirondelle ne fait pas le printemps: One swallow does not make a summer.

printemps	spring

Horloge (F)

une heure d'horloge   one solid hour

Nous en avons parlé pendant **deux heures d'horloge**: We talked about it for two solid hours.

horloge	clock

Huile (F)

une mer d'huile   a smooth sea, like a millpond

huile de coude   elbow grease

faire tache d'huile   to spread

Bien sûr ils vont s'en plaindre et cela **fera tache d'huile**, *vous verrez*: Of course they're going to complain about it, and it'll spread, you'll see.

huile	oil
tache	mark, stain

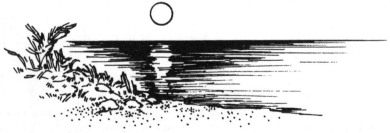

Une mer d'huile.

Iceberg (M)

Ce n'est que la partie émergée/visible de l'iceberg: It's just the tip of the iceberg.

Importer

n'importe no matter

Il n'est pas là? **N'importe:** He's not there? No matter.

dire/raconter n'importer quoi to talk nonsense, to talk through one's hat

Impossible

Impossible *n'est pas français:* There is no such word as impossible.

Impossible (M)

faire l'impossible pour faire quelque chose to make every effort to do something

J

Jamais

c'est le moment ou jamais   it's now or never

Jambe (F)

courir à toutes jambes   to run very fast, flat out

prendre ses jambes à son cou   to take to one's heels

cou	neck

Jeunesse (F)

ne plus être de la première jeunesse   to be getting on, to have seen better days

*Je monte dans un taxi qui **n'est plus de la première jeunesse**:* I get into a rather ancient taxi.

Joue (F)

tendre l'autre joue   to turn the other cheek

mettre quelqu'un en joue   to take aim at someone

*Il ouvre la porte et un policier **le met en joue**:* He opens the door and a policeman covers him with a gun.

Jouer

jouer gros	to play for high stakes
jouer serré	to play it tight, carefully
le temps joue/travaille pour nous	time is on our side
rien n'est encore joué	there is all to play for, nothing is decided yet
ce n'est pas joué d'avance	it isn't a foregone conclusion

Test Yourself!

PETITES REVISIONS 3
What is the missing word?

(Answers on page 128)

1. C'est un coup d'- - - - dans l'eau. (to be a useless gesture)
2. Les grands esprits se - - - -. (great minds think alike)
3. Je vais coucher à la belle - - - -. (to sleep out in the open)
4. Tout est prêt. On attend le - - - - vert. (to await the go-ahead)
5. On a fouillé le bâtiment de fond en - - - -. (from top to bottom)
6. J'ai dû faire contre mauvaise fortune bon - - -. (to put a brave face on things)
7. J'ai changé mon - - - - d'épaule. (to change one's ideas, to change tack)
8. Ils ont la gâchette - - - -. (to be trigger-happy)
9. Cela me va comme un - - - -. (to suit perfectly)
10. Un jour elle arrive sans crier - - - -. (without a word of warning)
11. Je l'implore mais elle est restée de - - - -. (to remain unmoved)
12. Le - - - - public. (the general public)
13. On joue à - - - - fermés. (to play to a full house)
14. Il courait à - - - - jambes. (to run flat out)
15. Le temps - - - - pour nous. (time is on our side)

Jour (M)

Ses jours sont comptés: His days are numbered.

ses vieux jours   one's old age

*Je garde cela pour **mes vieux jours:*** I am keeping that for my old age.

vivre au jour le jour   to live from day to day, to take each day as it comes

du jour au lendemain   overnight

***Du jour au lendemain** tout cela change:* Overnight all that changes.

le jour J   D-Day

Demain il fera jour: Tomorrow is another day.

Jurer

ne jurer que par quelque chose   to swear by something

Je ne jure que par cette méthode: I swear by this method.

il ne faut jurer de rien   you never can tell, you can't be sure of anything

L

Là

la question n'est pas là that's not the question, the point

*'"Pourquoi ces émissions n'ont-elles pas été détectées par la police? Peu importe. Pour l'instant, **la question n'est pas là**.'"* '"Why weren't these transmissions detected by the police? No matter. For the moment, that's not the point."' (*Les Six Compagnons et L'Emetteur Pirate*, Paul-Jacques Bonzon, Hachette Livre)

Laurier (M)

s'endormir sur ses lauriers to rest on one's laurels

Lendemain (M)

sans lendemain of short duration

des promesses sans lendemain promises which do not last long

les lendemains qui chantent a brighter, better future

*Ah oui, **les lendemains qui chantent**, ce n'est pas la première fois qu'on nous en parle!*: Ah yes, a brighter, better future, it's not the first time we've been told about that!

Lettre (F)

en toutes lettres   fully, clearly

Le document explique tout cela en toutes lettres: The document spells it all out very clearly.

Lieu (M)

avoir lieu   to take place

L'entrevue aura lieu la semaine prochaine: The interview will take place next week.

tenir lieu de   to serve as, to take the place of

Mon pardessus a tenu lieu de robe de chambre: My overcoat served as a dressing gown.

en haut lieu   in high places

Il prétend qu'il a des connaissances en haut lieu: He claims to know people in high places.

Lieue (F)

être à cent/mille lieues de penser   to be miles away from thinking

J'étais à mille lieues de penser qu'il allait démissionner: I never thought for a moment he was going to resign.

lieue	league (measurement)

Ligne (F)

les grandes lignes — the broad outline

Il nous a expliqué les grandes lignes de sa campagne: He explained to us the broad outline of his campaign.

la dernière ligne droite — the final stretch, final run-in, last bit

J'aurai bientôt fini d'écrire cette biographie. Je suis dans la dernière ligne droite: I'll soon have finished writing this biography. I'm on the final stretch.

Linge (M)

Il faut laver son linge sale en famille: You shouldn't wash your dirty linen in public.

Lire

dans l'attente de vous lire — looking forward to hearing from you (in a letter)

Loge (F)

être aux premières loges — to have a ringside seat

La bagarre continue sur le trottoir et les habitants des appartements, aux premières loges, ont tout vu: The brawl continues on the pavement and the people in the flats, with a grandstand view, saw everything.

loge	box (theatre)

Loi (F)

faire la loi to lay down the law, to rule the roost

Ici c'est les jeunes qui font la loi: Here it's the young who lay down the law.

Loin

mener loin to have far-reaching consequences

C'est un développement qui risque de mener loin: This is a development which could well have far-reaching consequences.

loin de moi l'idée de far be it from me to

Loin de moi l'idée de les critiquer: Far be it from me to criticise them.

mener	to lead

Long

de long en large up and down

Impatient il marche de long en large: He walks up and down impatiently.

en dire long to say a lot, to be very revealing

Ces statisques en disent long: These statistics are very revealing.

Son rire nerveux en dit long: His nervous laugh gives a lot away.

en savoir long to know a lot

Il y a ceux qui disent qu'il en sait long sur ce vol: There are those who say he knows a lot about this theft.

Longue (F)

à la longue   in the long run

A la longue leur patience va payer: In the long run their patience will pay off.

Longueur (F)

à longueur   throughout

A longueur d'année des chercheurs viennent travailler ici: Researchers come and work here throughout the year.

traîner en longueur   to drag on

des palabres qui traînent en longueur   talks which drag on

Louer

Dieu soit loué!   Heaven be praised!

Loup (M)

se jeter dans la gueule du loup   to jump into the lion's den

être connu comme le loup blanc   to be very well known, to be notorious

*La vieille dame au parapluie rouge? Elle est **connue comme le loup blanc**:* The old lady with the red umbrella? Everyone knows her.

à pas de loup   stealthily

'*Il poussa la petite porte de sa chambre mansardée et traversa le grenier à pas de loup.*' 'He pushed open the small door of his attic room and stealthily crossed the loft.' (*Le Printemps Viendra Deux Fois*, Claude Cénac, Hachette Livre)

gueule	mouth
loup	wolf

Lumière (F)

faire la lumière sur quelque chose   to clarify, to clear up something

C'est un mystère sur lequel je veux faire la lumière: It's a mystery I want to clear up.

lumière	light

Etre connu comme le loup blanc.

M

Machine (F)

faire machine/marche arrière to backtrack

Si vous pensez que le gouvernement va ***faire machine arrière*** *vous vous trompez:* If you think the government is going to backtrack you are mistaken.

machine	engine
marche arrière	reverse

Main (F)

la main dans la main hand in hand/hand in glove

mettre la dernière main à quelque chose to put the last touch to something

Je mets la dernière main à mon ***manuscrit****:* I'm putting the last touch to my manuscript.

donner un coup de main to give a helping hand

Il est toujours là pour lui ***donner un coup de main****:* He's always there to give her a helping hand.

j'en mettrais ma main au feu/à couper I'd stake my all on it

des deux mains enthusiastically

J'avoue qu'en ce cas-là j'aurais signé ***des deux mains****:* I admit that in that case I would have signed only too willingly.

Mal (M)

avoir du mal à faire quelque chose — to have difficulty in doing something

J'ai du mal à le faire comprendre: I have difficulty in making him understand.

prendre son mal en patience — to be patient about something

*Il y a un tout petit problème, m'explique-t-on. Je n'ai qu'à **prendre mon mal en patience**:* There is just a little problem, they explain. All I can do is be patient about it.

il n'y a pas de mal — there's no harm done, it is nothing to worry about

tant bien que mal — after a fashion, as best one can

*Alors j'ai écrit deux poèmes **tant bien que mal** que je lui ai envoyés:* So I wrote two poems as best I could, which I sent to her.

Malheur (M)

Ne parlez pas de malheur!: Heaven forbid! Don't tempt fate!

malheur	misfortune

Marteau (M)

entre le marteau et l'enclume — between the devil and the deep blue sea

*Si je dis la vérité je risque d'être accusé. Je suis **entre le marteau et l'enclume**:* If I tell the truth I risk being accused. I'm between the devil and the deep blue sea.

marteau	hammer
enclume	anvil

Masque (M)

jeter le masque to reveal one's true colours, one's real self

Même

Cela revient au même: That comes to the same thing.

Mémoire (F)

de mémoire d'homme in living memory

De mémoire d'étudiant on n'a jamais connu cela: No student has ever known that to happen.

Merci

Dieu merci!: Thank Heaven!

Meuble (M)

sauver les meubles to save something from the wreckage

Si le Premier ministre veut **sauver les meubles** il lui faut agir vite – d'abord il doit tout nier: If the Prime Minister wants to save something from the wreckage he must act quickly – first he must deny everything.

meubles	furniture

Mieux

tant mieux!　　　　　　　　　so much the better!

Albert ne peut pas venir. **Tant mieux** *puisque je lui dois encore de l'argent:* Albert can't come. That's good because I still owe him some money.

faire de son mieux　　　　　　to do one's best

*Je ne sais pas si je peux vous aider mais je **ferai de mon mieux**:* I don't know if I can help you but I'll do my best.

faute de mieux　　　　　　　　for want of anything better

*Je le prendrai **faute de mieux**:* I'll take it if there's nothing else.

Mine (F)

ne pas payer de mine　　　　not to be much to look at

*Au bout de la rue il y avait un petit café qui **ne payait pas de mine**:* At the end of the road was a little café which didn't look up to much.

mine	appearance

Moindre

*Devant la gare il n'y avait pas le **moindre** taxi:* There wasn't a single taxi at the station.

c'est la moindre des choses　it's nothing, don't mention it

et non des moindres　　　　　important ones too

*Plusieurs auteurs – **et non des moindres** – ont écrit une lettre pour protester:* Several authors – important ones too – have written a letter to protest.

Monde (M)

depuis que le monde est monde	since the world began, since the beginning of time
il y a du monde	there are a lot of people
on refuse du monde	people are being turned away

*De tels conflits internationaux existent **depuis que le monde est monde**:* There have been international conflicts like this as far back as you can go.

Monnaie (F)

c'est monnaie courante	it's commonplace, par for the course

*Hélas, de tels actes de vandalisme sont devenus **monnaie courante**:* Alas, such acts of vandalism have become commonplace.

monnaie	currency

Mont (M)

être par monts et par vaux	to be up and away, on the move

*Mais dites-moi, quand vous êtes **par monts et par vaux** en Europe chaque été, qui s'occupe des enfants?:* But tell me, when you're moving round Europe every summer, who looks after the children?

mont	mountain
val	valley

Montre (F)

la course contre la montre	race against time
jouer la montre	to play for time

*Je ne veux pas dévoiler les noms, alors **je joue la montre**:* I don't want to give away the names so I play for time.

Mort (M)

faire le mort	to lie low

mort	dead man

Mot (M)

en un mot	in a nutshell, in a word
écrire un mot à quelqu'un	to drop someone a line

***Un petit mot pour vous dire** que tout va bien:* Just a line to let you know that all is well.

dire deux mots à quelqu'un	to have a (sharp) word with someone

*'"Quant à celui qui m'a joué ce tour . . . **je vais aller lui dire deux mots**."'* '"As for the person who played this trick on me . . . I'm going to have a word with him."' (*Les Etranges Vacances de Michel*, Georges Bayard, Hachette Livre)

Mouchoir (M)

grand comme un mouchoir de poche   tiny, minute

une pelouse grande comme un mouchoir de poche   a tiny lawn

Mur (M)

être au pied du mur   to be driven into a corner, to be forced into a decision

se heurter à un mur   to come up against a brick wall

*Mais dans le village personne ne voulait en parler. On **s'est heurté à un mur**:* But in the village nobody would talk about it. We came up against a brick wall.

| *heurter* | to hit, to strike |

N

Nature

nature   with nothing added

'Des framboises?' *'Oui, s'il vous plaît,* **nature.***'*: 'Some raspberries?' 'Yes please, just on their own.'

Nature (F)

plus grand que nature   larger than life

un village plus suisse que nature   a village too typically Swiss to be true

Neuf

quoi de neuf?   what's new? what's the news?

Noeud (M)

le noeud de l'affaire   the crux of the matter

noeud	knot

Noir

un point noir   a drawback

Un point noir, *le service après-vente laisse à désirer:* A drawback is that the after-sales service leaves something to be desired.

Nouveau

ne pas être chose nouvelle   to be nothing new

*De telles accusations **ne sont pas chose nouvelle**:* There's nothing new about such accusations.

tout nouveau, tout beau   wait until the novelty wears off

Nuage (M)

sans nuage(s)   serene, unblemished

*Leur vie ensemble a été **sans nuage**:* Their life together has been perfect.

nuage	cloud

Nuit (F)

***Il fait nuit noire**:* It's pitch black.

<u>Nez</u>   Don't cut off your nose
to spite your face.

Ne sciez pas la branche sur
laquelle vous êtes assis.

O

Oeil (M)

jeter un coup d'oeil à/sur   to glance at

*Elle **jette un coup d'oeil sur** le baromètre:* She glances at the barometer.

voir quelque chose d'un bon oeil   to look kindly on something

*Ses parents **ne voient pas ce voyage d'un bon oeil**:* His parents don't look kindly on this trip.

fermer les yeux (sur)   to turn a blind eye (to)

*Au lieu d'accuser son fils elle préfère **fermer les yeux**:* Instead of accusing her son, she prefers to turn a blind eye.

sauter aux yeux   to be evident, to stand out clearly

*On a dépensé beaucoup d'argent ici, cela **saute aux yeux**:* A lot of money has been spent here, that's very obvious.

Oeuf (M)

étouffer/tuer dans l'oeuf   to nip in the bud

étouffer	to stifle

Ombre (F)

il y une ombre au tableau   there's a snag, drawback, a fly in the ointment

*Seule **ombre au tableau**: on arrivera à son hôtel après minuit:* Just one snag, you won't get to your hotel until after midnight.

ombre	shadow

Or (M)

valoir son pesant d'or   to be worth one's/its weight in gold

faire des affaires d'or   to rake in the money, to make a mint

une occasion en or pour   a golden opportunity to

parler d'or   to speak words of wisdom

des gens en or   super people

Oreille (F)

faire la sourde oreille   to turn a deaf ear

dresser/tendre l'oreille   to prick up one's ears

'*Tous les six, nous avions **tendu l'oreille** et, naturellement, la même idée nous était venue.*' 'All six of us had pricked up our ears and, naturally, the same idea had occurred to us.' (*Les Six Compagnons et L'Homme des Neiges*, Paul-Jacques Bonzon, Hachette Livre)

ne pas l'entendre ce cette oreille   not to see it that way, not to agree

*La directrice **ne l'entend pas de cette oreille**:* The headmistress doesn't see it that way.

O*s* (M)

mouillé/trempé jusqu'aux os   soaked through

os	bone

O*ubliettes* (F)

tomber dans les oubliettes   to be forgotten, to be put on one side

*Pourvu que son beau plan **ne tombe pas dans les oubliettes**!:* Let's hope his fine plan isn't just forgotten!

oubliettes	dungeon

O*ui* (M)

pour un oui, pour un non   at the drop of a hat

***Pour un oui ou un non** elle fond en larmes de joie:* She bursts into tears of joy at the drop of a hat.

O*urs* (M)

tourner comme un ours en cage   to pace up and down like a caged animal

ours	bear

P

Panne (F)

tomber en panne   to break down

La voiture tombe en panne: The car breaks down.

Le taxi est en panne d'essence: The taxi has run out of petrol.

*Si par mauvais temps vous êtes **en panne d'idée**, pourquoi ne pas visiter nos musées?*: If the weather is bad and you don't know what to do, why not look around our museums?

Papier (M)

sur le papier   on paper

*'Est-ce qu'ils vont gagner?' 'Je ne sais pas, mais **sur le papier** ils sont beaucoup plus forts.'*: 'Will they win?' 'I don't know, but on paper they're much stronger.'

Parcours (M)

le parcours du combattant   a veritable obstacle course

*Pour y arriver j'ai dû changer de train trois fois avant de prendre le car. Un véritable **parcours du combattant**!*: To get there I had to change trains three times before catching the bus. A real obstacle course!

parcours du combattant	assault course

Paroisse (F)

prêcher pour sa paroisse to be concerned about one's own interests, to have an axe to grind

paroisse	parish

Parole (F)

n'avoir qu'une parole to be true to one's word

*Vous me connaissez bien, **je n'ai qu'une parole**:* You know me well, I am a man of my word.

Pas (M)

revenir sur ses pas to retrace one's steps

faire les cent pas to pace up and down

marquer le pas to mark time, to pause

*Ce n'est que **le premier pas** qui coûte:* It's just the beginning which is difficult, it's easy once you've made a start.

Patte (F)

à quatre pattes on all fours

patte	leg, paw

Peau (F)

faire peau neuve   to turn over a new leaf

peau	skin

Pédale (F)

mettre la pédale douce   to soft-pedal

C'est une politique que les gens vont détester. C'est le moment de **mettre la pédale douce** *à mon avis:* It's a policy which people are going to hate. In my opinion, it's the moment to soft-pedal.

Peigne (M)

passer au peigne fin   to go through with a fine toothcomb

La police va **passer** *le jardin de l'accusé* **au peigne fin:** The police are going to examine the accused's garden in minute detail.

Pencher

se pencher sur   to look carefully at, to consider

Le directeur va **se pencher sur** *ce problème:* The chairman is going to examine this problem.

se pencher	to lean, to bend

Pendule (F)

remettre les pendules à l'heure	to put the record straight

pendule	clock

On ne peut pas retarder les pendules – you can't turn back the clock

Pente (F)

remonter la pente	to climb back, to recover

*J'allais la voir chaque jour. Je l'ai aidée à **remonter la pente**:* I used to go and see her every day. I helped her to get back on her feet.

pente	slope

Père (M)

un placement de père de famille	a safe and sound investment

Petit

petit à petit	bit by bit, gradually
une petite heure	scarcely an hour

*Elle a prévu **une petite heure** pour le terminer:* She reckoned it needed an hour to finish it, if that.

Petit (M)

faire des petits   to grow (money)

*Vous voulez que votre argent **fasse des petits**? Ecrivez-nous!:* You want your money to grow? Write to us!

Peu

peu à peu   bit by bit, gradually

***Peu à peu** je m'y habitue:* I'm gradually getting used to it.

d'ici peu   before long

***D'ici peu** toute l'équipe parlera un peu de français:* Before long the whole team will speak a bit of French.

***Pour un peu** je l'aurais mis à la porte:* For two pins I would have shown him the door.

***Un peu plus** il me renversait:* He very nearly knocked me over.

Pied (M)

pied à pied   every inch of the way

*Ils se battent **pied à pied**:* They are fighting every inch of the way.

mettre quelque chose sur pied   to set something up

*Ensemble nous avons **mis sur pied** cet échange entre les deux pays:* Together we set up this exchange between the two countries.

partir du mauvais pied   to get off to a bad start

*Nous somme **partis du mauvais pied**. Ce n'est que maintenant que les affaires marchent:* We got off to a bad start. It's only now that business is good.

faire des pieds et des mains pour faire quelque chose   to make a great effort to do something

pieds et poings liés   bound hand and foot

retomber sur ses pieds   to fall on one's feet

*Il a de la chance; il **retombe** toujours **sur ses pieds**:* He's lucky; he always falls on his feet

avoir les pieds sur terre   to have one's feet on the ground

*Il faut avoir de l'imagination, mais surtout il faut **avoir les pieds sur terre**:* You need imagination, but above all you must have your feet on the ground.

perdre pied   to be out of one's depth

*On commence à parler informatique. **Je perds pied**:* They begin to talk computers. I'm out of my depth.

les pieds dans l'eau   on the waterfront, right by the water's edge

un restaurant les pieds dans l'eau   a restaurant right by the water's edge

avoir bon pied bon oeil   to be hale and hearty

*Grand-père a toujours **bon pied bon oeil**:* Grandfather is still hale and hearty.

poing	fist

Un restaurant les pieds dans l'eau.

Test Yourself!

PETITES REVISIONS 4
What is the missing word?

(Answers on page 128)

1. Ses jours sont - - - -. (his days are numbered)
2. Les lendemains qui - - - - -. (a brighter, better future)
3. Il traverse la pelouse à pas de - - - -. (to walk stealthily)
4. Ne parlez pas de - - - ! (to tempt fate)
5. Malheureusement je me trouve entre le - - - - et l'enclume. (to be between the devil and the deep blue sea)
6. En un - - - -. (in a nutshell)
7. Le - - - - de l'affaire. (the crux of the matter)
8. Il fait nuit - - - -. (to be pitch black)
9. Un scandale qu'ils ont vite tué dans l'- - - -. (to nip in the bud)
10. Mais il y a une - - - - au tableau. (to be a snag, a fly in the ointment)
11. Je suis mouillé jusqu'aux - - - -. (to be soaked through)
12. Vous prêchez pour votre - - - - -. (to have an axe to grind)
13. Il fait les - - - pas. (to pace up and down)
14. On dit qu'il a fait - - - - neuve. (to turn over a new leaf)
15. Ils se battent pied à - - - - - (every inch of the way)

Pied
=

Bon pied, bon oeuil
As fit as a fiddle

Pierre (F)

un placement pierre an investment in bricks and mortar, in property

faire d'une pierre deux coups to kill two birds with one stone

Pignon (M)

avoir pignon sur rue to be accepted, well established

*Ce jeune chef a maintenant **pignon sur rue** dans les beaux quartiers de la ville:* This young chef is now well established in the smart part of the town.

pignon	gable

Pilule (F)

dorer la pilule to sugar the pill

*Je dois aller travailler en centre-ville. Ah! le bruit! Et la circulation! Mais on **m'a doré la pilule** en me disant que mon bureau sera plus confortable:* I have to go and work in the town centre. Oh! the noise! And the traffic! But they have sugared the pill by telling me that my office will be more comfortable.

avaler la pilule to bite the bullet

*Mon premier livre a eu du succès, mais lorsque mon éditeur a rejeté mon deuxième livre j'ai dû **avaler la pilule**:* My first book was a success, but when my publisher turned down my second book I had to put up with it.

dorer	to gild
avaler	to swallow

Pirouette (F)

s'en tirer par une pirouette   to sidestep a question neatly

*Le Premier ministre **s'en tire par une pirouette**:* The Prime Minister neatly sidesteps the question.

Pis

tant pis!   too bad! so much the worse!

*Maintenant il a peur de manquer son examen. **Tant pis**, il aurait dû écouter ses professeurs:* Now he's afraid of failing his exam. Too bad, he should have listened to his teachers.

Place (F)

à votre place   if I were you

sur la place publique   in public, out in the open

*Espérons qu'on ne va pas porter cette affaire **sur la place publique**:* Let's hope this matter is not going to be aired in public.

place	(town) square

Plaire

Plaît-il?   I beg your pardon? What did you say?

Plomb (M)

un sommeil de plomb	heavy, deep sleep
un soleil de plomb	brilliant sunshine

plomb	lead

Pluie (F)

parler de la pluie et du beau temps	to make small talk

*On y arrive, on accepte un verre, **on parle de la pluie et du beau temps**:* You arrive, you take a drink, you make small talk.

Poche

connaître comme sa poche	to know like the back of one's hand

*Ne vous inquiétez pas, **je connais cette ville comme ma poche**:* Don't worry, I know this town like the back of my hand.

poche	pocket

Poids (M)

faire le poids	to measure up

*Malgré sa réputation et son expérience on se demande s'il **fera le poids** face à son rival:* In spite of his reputation and experience one wonders whether he'll be up to it when faced by his rival.

poids	weight

Poire (F)

couper la poire en deux   to split the difference, to share out equally

garder une poire pour la soif   to put something by for a rainy day

Oui, j'ai mis de l'argent à côté. **Une poire pour la soif**: Yes, I've put some money on one side. Something for a rainy day.

Poisson (M)

être comme un poisson dans l'eau   to feel perfectly at home

Pomme (F)

pomme de discorde   bone of contention

Pont (M)

faire le pont   to stop over, to make a long weekend of it (for example, following a Bank Holiday)

Jeudi c'est la fête de l'Ascension et **je ferai le pont** *comme tout le monde*: Thursday is Ascension Day and I'll make a long weekend of it like everyone else.

couper les ponts   to break off contact, to break off relations

On espère tout de même que l'Angleterre ne va pas **couper les ponts** *avec ces deux pays*: All the same, one hopes that England is not going to break off relations with these two countries.

Port (M)

arriver à bon port	to make it home safely, to get there in the end
échouer près du port	to fall at the last hurdle

échouer	to go aground

Porte (F)

journée portes ouvertes	open day

La **journée portes ouvertes** *a été repoussée à l'hiver:* The open day has been put back to the winter.

balayer devant sa porte	to put one's own house in order (before criticising others)

Ce que j'en pense, moi? Je pense qu'ils exagèrent et qu'ils devraient **balayer devant leur porte** *avant de nous accuser:* What do I think? I think they're exaggerating and ought to put their own house in order before accusing us.

balayer	to sweep

Position (F)

camper/rester sur ses positions to stick to one's guns

Les étudiants **restent sur leurs positions***:* The students are sticking to their guns.

Pot (M)

tourner autour du pot   to beat about the bush

*Cette fois elle n'a pas **tourné autour du pot**. 'D'où vient cet argent?'
a-t-elle demandé brusquement:* This time she didn't beat about the bush.
'Where did you get this money?' she asked sharply.

Poudre (F)

se répandre comme une   to spread like wildfire
traînée de poudre

*'La nouvelle **se répandit comme une traînée de poudre** et
déchaîna presque une liesse populaire, tant le mercenaire nazi était
craint et haï.'* 'The news spread like wildfire and aroused a feeling of
almost popular rejoicing, so feared and hated was the Nazi hireling.' (*La
Résistance Normande Face à la Gestapo*, Raymond Ruffin, Presses de la
Cité)

traînée	trail

Poule (F)

tuer la poule aux oeufs d'or   to kill the goose that lays the
golden egg

poule	hen

Pouls (M)

prende le pouls   to sound out

*Pour commencer je vais **prendre le pouls** des universités:* To start with
I'm going to see how the universities feel.

pouls	pulse

Poumon (M)

crier à pleins poumons	to shout out with all one's might
respirer à pleins poumons	to breathe in deeply

poumon	lung

Pour (M)

le pour et le contre	the pros and cons

*Avant d'agir il faut toujours peser **le pour et le contre**:* Before acting one must always weigh up the pros and cons.

Pouvoir

on ne peut plus	greatly, extremely
un roman on ne peut plus passionnant	a most exciting novel

Prendre

à tout prendre	on the whole, all in all

*Mes élèves sont **à tout prendre** très polis:* On the whole, my pupils are very polite.

Preuve (F)

faire ses preuves

to prove oneself/itself, to show what one can do, to show one's mettle, to win one's spurs

*Ce jeune officier a bientôt **fait ses preuves***: This young officer soon showed what he could do.

Prince (M)

les princes qui nous gouvernent

our rulers, those in charge

être bon prince

to be a generous sort

*L'Etat, **bon prince**, va les rembourser:* In a generous gesture, the state will pay them back.

Prix (M)

à tout prix

at any cost

être dans ses prix

to be in one's price range

*J'espère que je trouverai quelque chose **dans mes prix***: I hope I'll find something in my price range.

Q

Quart (M)

les trois-quarts du temps   most of the time

Les trois-quarts du temps *il lit chez lui au lieu d'aller jouer avec ses camarades:* Most of the time he reads at home instead of going to play with his friends.

Que

que de   what a lot

que de gens!   what a lot of people!

que faire?   what is to be done?

ne savoir que faire   not to know what to do

'*Furieux, et en même temps effrayés, les SS pris de panique **ne savent que faire** de tous leurs prisonniers qui risquent de s'enfuir.*' 'Furious, and at the same time frightened, the panic-stricken SS don't know what to do with all their prisoners, who could well escape.' (*La Résistance Normande Face à la Gestapo,* Raymond Ruffin, Presses de la Cité)

Il ne sait que faire.

Queue (F)

n'avoir ni queue ni tête   to be incomprehensible

*Cette histoire devient de plus en plus compliquée. Elle **n'a ni queue
ni tête**:* This story gets more and more complicated. You can't make head
or tail of it.

la queue basse   with one's tail between one's
legs

*Il rougit un peu, murmure quelque chose et part **la queue basse**:* He
blushes a little, mutters something and leaves with his tail between his legs.

queue	tail

Quoi

il n'y a pas de quoi   don't mention it

*'Merci d'y avoir pensé.' '**Il n'y a pas de quoi.**':* 'Thanks for thinking of
it.' 'Don't mention it.'

R

Rat (M)

être fait comme un rat   to be caught (like a rat in a trap)

*Soudain il y a des soldats partout. Il **est fait comme un rat**:* Suddenly there are soldiers everywhere. He is completely trapped.

Recette (F)

faire recette   to be a success, to work out well, to pay off

*L'idée de devenir une ville de congrès a **fait recette**:* The idea of becoming a conference town has been a success.

recette	takings

Il est fait comme un rat.

Réflexion (F)

**cela donne matière à
réflexion**

that gives you food for thought

Ride (F)

ne pas prendre une ride

to be as good as ever, to show
no signs of age, to be as smooth
as ever

*Même aujourd'hui on entend sa musique partout. Ses compositions
n'ont pas pris une ride:* Even today you hear his music everywhere.
His compositions show no sign of age.

ride	wrinkle

Rimer

rimer avec

to be the same as

*Il a gagné Wimbledon trois fois. Pour les gens de mon âge son nom
rime avec tennis:* He won Wimbledon three times. For people of my age,
his name and tennis are synonymous.

Hélas, Noël ne rime pas toujours avec bonheur: Unfortunately
Christmas and happiness do not always go together.

cela ne rime à rien

it makes no sense, it's pointless,
it doesn't add up

*On refuse de nous l'expliquer ou de nous dire ce qui se passe. Mais
pourquoi ce silence? Cela ne rime à rien:* They refuse to explain it to
us or tell us what is happening. But why this silence? It makes no sense at
all.

Rire

il n'y a pas de quoi rire   it's no laughing matter

Ils ont fait cela pour rire: They did it for a laugh.

Il l'a pris en riant: He laughed it off.

Romain (M)

un travail de Romain   a Herculean task

romain	Roman

Rose (F)

durer ce que durent les roses   to be short-lived, not to last long, to be quick to fade

*C'est un projet très ambitieux qui risque de **durer ce que durent les roses***: It's a very ambitious project which is not likely to last long.

Roue (F)

être la cinquième roue du carrosse   to be superfluous, of no importance

*Mais ici, malgré mon expérience, **je ne suis que la cinquième roue du carrosse***: But here, in spite of my experience, I'm worthless.

roue	wheel
carrosse	coach, carriage

Rouge

le téléphone rouge

hot line (as between superpowers)

Route (F)

faire fausse route

to bark up the wrong tree

Rue (F)

l'homme de la rue

the man in the street

Et l'homme de la rue? Qu'est-ce qu'il va en penser? C'est là la question: And the man in the street? What will he think about it? That's the question.

ne pas courir les rues

to be uncommon, rare

La galanterie ne court pas les rues: Acts of chivalry are rare.

De tels héros ne courent pas les rues: Such heroes are rare.

S

Sac (M)

mettre dans le même sac to lump together

*Quant aux criminels, elle les **met tous dans le même sac**:* As for criminals, she lumps them all together.

Saint (M)

le Saint des Saints the Holy of Holies

*Pour la première fois j'entre dans **le Saint des Saints**:* For the first time I enter the Holy of Holies.

ne pas savoir à quel saint se vouer not to know which way to turn, to be at one's wits' end

se vouer	to devote oneself, to dedicate oneself

Salle (F)

faire salle comble to play to a full house, to be packed out

une salle noire qui fait salle comble a cinema which is packed out

Salut (M)

chercher son salut dans la fuite to seek safety in flight

Test Yourself!

PETITES REVISIONS 5
What is the missing word?

(Answers on page 128)

1. J'ai fait d'une pierre deux - - - -. (to kill two birds with one stone)
2. Ils ont essayé de - - - - la pilule. (to sugar the pill)
3. J'ai dû - - - - la pilule. (to bite the bullet)
4. Je connais cette ville comme ma - - -. (to know like the back of one's hand)
5. Elle n'a pas oublié de garder une - - - - pour la soif. (to put something by for a rainy day)
6. C'est une - - - de discorde. (to be a bone of contention)
7. Ils - - - - sur leurs positions. (to stick to one's guns)
8. Il est parti la queue - - - - . (with one's tail between one's legs)
9. Il n'y a pas de - - - - . (don't mention it)
10. Cela donne - - - - - à réflexion. (to be food for thought)
11. Je suis la cinquième roue du - - - - - -. (to be superfluous)
12. De tels héros ne courent pas les - - - -. (to be rare)
13. Elle les a mis dans le même - - - -. (to lump together)
14. Je ne sais pas à quel - - - me vouer. (not to know which way to turn)
15. Je cherche mon - - - - - dans la fuite. (to seek safety in flight)

Sauce (F)

mettre (un mot) à toutes les sauces

to use (a word) in all sorts of ways, in a general and vague sense

*'Client' devient **un de ces mots qu'on met à toutes les sauces**:* 'Customer' is becoming one of those words you can just use any old how.

Semelle (F)

ne pas quitter quelqu'un d'une semelle

to stick closely to someone, to dog someone's footsteps

| *semelle* | sole (shoe) |

Sénateur (M)

un train de sénateur

a stately pace

*La gondole louée, nous avançons **à un train de sénateur**, pour mieux admirer Venise:* Having hired a gondola, we proceed at a stately pace, the better to admire Venice.

Sentier (M)

hors des sentiers battus

off the beaten track

des vacances hors des sentiers battus

holidays off the beaten track

| *sentier* | path |

Signe (M)

signes extérieurs (de richesse) status symbols

Sa maison est modeste, sa voiture est vieille. **Les signes extérieurs de richesse** *ne l'intéressent pas du tout:* His house is a modest one, his car is old. Status symbols do not interest him at all.

Situation (F)

l'homme de la situation just the man for the job

Tout le monde est sûr qu'il se révèlera **l'homme de la situation***:* Everybody is sure he will prove to be the right man for the job.

Des signes extérieurs de richesse.

Sonnant

à onze heures sonnantes right on eleven

'A dix heures sonnantes, nous débarquons devant la gare.' 'At ten on the dot, we roll up at the station.' (*Les Six Compagnons et L'Homme des Neiges*, Paul-Jacques Bonzon, Hachette Livre)

Souhait (M)

à souhait(s) extremely, perfectly

un steak tendre à souhait a beautifully tender steak

souhait	wish

Sourire (M)

garder le sourire to keep smiling

Sueur (F)

à la sueur de son front by the sweat of one's brow

*J'ai gagné cet argent **à la sueur de mon front**, chaque sou:* I earned this money by the sweat of my brow, every penny of it.

Suffrage (M)

rallier tous les suffrages to win universal approval

*Son court métrage **a rallié tous les suffrages**:* His short film won universal acclaim.

suffrage	vote

T

Taille (F)

de taille   large, considerable

*C'est un argument **de taille***: It's a powerful argument.

taille	size

Tailleur (M)

être assis en tailleur   to sit cross-legged

***Assis en tailleur** sur le sol, il nous raconte son aventure:* Sitting cross-legged on the ground, he tells us about his adventure.

tailleur	tailor

Tambour (M)

sans tambour ni trompette   quietly, discreetly, without fuss

*Lorsque le scandale éclate ici il part pour l'Amérique **sans tambour ni trompette***: When the scandal breaks here, he slips quietly away to America.

tambour	drum

Tapis (M)

le tapis rouge the red carpet

*On a déployé **le tapis rouge** pour les accueillir:* We put out the red carpet to welcome them.

mettre sur le tapis to bring up for discussion, to air

*Notre prochaine réunion sera en mars et on m'a demandé de **mettre ce problème sur le tapis**:* Our next meeting is in March and I have been asked to bring this problem up for discussion.

tapis	table cover

Temps (M)

de temps en temps/à autre from time to time

avoir tout son temps to have plenty of time

Nous avons tout notre temps: We have ample time.

en temps utile/voulu in due course

*Elle le fera **en temps utile**:* She will do it in due course.

le bon vieux temps the good old days

vivre/marcher avec le temps to move with the times

avoir fait son temps to have had one's/its day

*Mon vieux chapeau de paille **a fait son temps**:* My old straw hat has had its day.

il est grand temps de/que it is high time to/that/for

*'Les paras du major Howard tiennent toujours les ponts, mais **il est grand temps que** les renforts arrivent.'* 'Major Howard's paras are still holding the bridges, but it's high time for the reinforcements to arrive.' (*Résistance Normande et Jour J*, Raymond Ruffin, Presses de la Cité)

Tenir

Un tiens vaut mieux que deux tu l'auras: A bird in the hand is worth two in the bush.

Terrain (M)

tâter le terrain   to feel one's way

*Pour le moment **je tâte le terrain**, c'est tout:* For the moment I'm putting out a few feelers, that's all.

trouver un terrain d'entente   to find common ground

*L'important c'est de **trouver un terrain d'entente**. Je suis optimiste car nous sommes du même parti:* The important thing is to find some common ground. I am optimistic as our politics are the same.

ne pas suivre quelqu'un   not to go along with someone
sur ce terrain   on that point

*Vous êtes plus tolérant que moi. **Je ne vous suis pas sur ce terrain:*** You're more tolerant than I am. I can't go along with you on that.

Terre (F)

être terre-à-terre   to be down to earth

Tête (F)

tomber la tête la première   to fall head first

avoir la tête sur les épaules   to be level-headed

garder la tête hors de l'eau   to keep one's head above water

*Ce n'est pas facile. C'est tout juste si **je garde la tête hors de l'eau:*** It's not easy. I'm only just keeping my head above water.

avoir la tête de l'emploi   to look the part

*Ah, voilà le chef qui entre. **Il a la tête de l'emploi**, n'est-ce pas?:* Ah there's the chef coming in. He looks the part, doesn't he?

Toit (M)

crier sur les toits　　　　to cry out from the rooftops

*Moi, aussi, j'ai eu une enfance malheureuse mais je ne vais pas le **crier sur les toits**:* I, too, had an unhappy childhood but I'm not going to broadcast it.

Ton (M)

répéter sur tous les tons　　to repeat over and over again

*On nous **répète sur tous les tons** ce qu'il faut faire en cas d'incendie:* We're told again and again what to do in case of fire.

Tortue (F)

à pas de tortue　　　　at a snail's pace

tortue	tortoise

Tout (M)

tenter le tout pour le tout　to risk everything, to stake one's all

le tout est de　　　　the important thing is to

Le tout est de répondre aux questions sans hésiter: The important thing is to answer the questions without hesitating.

Trait d'union (M)

servir de trait d'union   to act as a go-between

*Tout le monde le respecte et je crois bien qu'il pourrait servir de **trait d'union** entre le gouvernement et les syndicats:* Everybody respects him and I really think he could act as a go-between between the government and the unions.

trait d'union	hyphen

Tranchant (M)

à double tranchant   double-edged

*C'est un argument **à double tranchant:*** It cuts both ways.

tranchant	cutting edge

Tu

être à tu et à toi avec   to be on familiar, very friendly
quelqu'un   terms with someone

*L'aubergiste **est à tu et à toi avec ses fidèles**:* My host is on very friendly terms with his regulars.

U

Unanimité (F)

faire l'unanimité   to find universal favour

*Sa proposition n'a pas **fait l'unanimité**:* His proposal was not accepted by everyone.

Utile (M)

joindre l'utile à l'agréable   to mix business with pleasure

*Quand vous viendrez chez nous en juillet pour le congrès n'oubliez pas d'apporter votre raquette de tennis pour que vous puissiez **joindre l'utile à l'agréable**:* When you come to us in July for the conference don't forget your tennis racket so you can mix business and pleasure.

V

Vache (F)

le temps des vaches maigres   lean times

C'est **le temps des vaches maigres** pour l'industrie: These are lean times for industry.

Vaisseau (M)

brûler ses vaisseaux   to burn one's boats

En mettant cela par écrit **il a brûlé ses vaisseaux**: By putting it in writing he has burnt his boats.

Vapeur (F)

renverser la vapeur   to backtrack, to stop, to change course

Il ne s'agit pas d'une crise et il n'est pas question de **renverser la vapeur**, nous assure le ministre: There's no crisis and there's no question of backtracking, the minister assures us.

vapeur	steam

Va-tout (M)

jouer son va-tout   to risk all, to gamble everything, to go for broke

Venir

premier venu   just any/any old

Je ne vais pas manger dans le premier hôtel venu: I'm not going to eat in just any hotel.

L'officier qui est venu nous parler n'était pas le premier venu. C'est un héros de guerre: The officer who came to speak to us wasn't just anyone. He's a war hero.

voir venir   to await events

Ils préfèrent voir venir: They prefer to wait and see what's going to happen.

Vent (M)

prendre le vent   to see which way the wind is
                                     blowing, to see how the land lies

contre vents et marées   through thick and thin/against
                                     the odds

Il a non seulement réussi mais il l'a fait contre vents et marées: Not only has he succeeded, but he has done so against all the odds.

marée	tide

Ventre (M)

courir ventre à terre   to run flat out, to tear along

ventre	stomach

Ver (M)

le ver est entré dans le fruit the rot has set in

C'est un joueur invétéré. **Le ver est entré dans le fruit** *le jour de son quinzième anniversaire où il a misé sur un cheval pour la première fois:* He's an inveterate gambler. The trouble started on the day of his fifteenth birthday when he bet on a horse for the first time.

ver	worm

Vérité (F)

la minute de vérité the moment of truth

C'est difficilement explicable, mais plus **la minute de vérité** *approche, moins j'ai peur:* It's hard to explain, but the closer the moment of truth comes, the less afraid I am.

criant de vérité lifelike

Le policier m'a montré un faux billet **criant de vérité**: The policeman showed me a forged note which looked absolutely genuine.

Il court ventre à terre.

Verre (M)

se noyer dans un verre d'eau   to get into a state about small problems, to flounder, to create a storm in a teacup

Impossible de le promouvoir. Il manque d'assurance. **Il se noie dans un verre d'eau***:* Impossible to promote him. He lacks confidence. He gets into a state over the smallest problems.

se noyer	to drown

Vert

numéro vert   freephone number

Attendez, il y a **un numéro vert***. Je vous le cherche:* Wait, there's a freephone number. I'll get it for you.

Vinaigre (M)

tourner au vinaigre   to turn sour

Mais ce plaisir inattendu **tourne bientôt au vinaigre***:* But this unexpected pleasure soon turns sour.

vinaigre	vinegar

Violon (M)

accorder ses violons   to come to general agreement

Il n'y a pas de temps à perdre. Il faut que le conseil **accorde ses violons** *sans tarder:* There is no time to lose. The committee must come to an agreement without delay.

aller plus vite que les violons/la musique   to go too fast, to jump the gun

Mais **vous allez plus vite que les violons***! On ne peut rien faire sans preuves!:* But you're jumping the gun! We can't do anything without proof!

Visage (M)

à visage découvert openly

*Il est non seulement important qu'il s'en occupe tout de suite mais encore qu'il agisse **à visage découvert**:* It is not only important that he deals with it at once, but that he also acts openly.

Vivre

prendre le temps de vivre to stand back and enjoy life, to take time to relax

avoir vécu to have had its day/to be a thing of the past

*La punition d'être mis au pain et à l'eau **a vécu**:* The punishment of being on bread and water is a thing of the past.

Voeu (M)

voeu(x) pieux wishful thinking

*Je sais ce qu'ils veulent faire. Mais il leur faudrait des armes sophistiquées qu'ils n'ont pas. C'est un **voeu pieux**:* I know what they want to do. But they would need sophisticated weapons which they don't have. It's wishful thinking.

voeu	wish
pieux	pious

Voie (F)

la voie est libre the way is open, the coast is clear

passer par la voie hiérarchique to go through the official channels

Voiler

se voiler la face to avert one's eyes

*Au lieu de **se voiler la face** il faut reconnaître que la délinquance juvénile est toujours un gros problème:* Instead of ignoring it, one must recognise that juvenile delinquency is still a big problem.

voiler	to veil

Voir

c'est à voir it remains to be seen, we shall see

*Elle a promis de ne pas recommencer. **C'est à voir**:* She's promised not to do it again. We shall see.

n'avoir rien à voir avec not to have anything to do with

*Cela **n'a rien à voir** avec cette dispute:* That has nothing to do with this quarrel.

Vouloir

que voulez-vous? what do you expect?

*Mais **que veux-tu**? Ces gamins n'ont jamais connu leur père:* But what do you expect? These kids never knew their father.

vouloir c'est pouvoir where there's a will there's a way

Z

Zéro (M)

repartir à zéro   to start again from scratch

L'enquête piétine. Il nous faudra **repartir à zéro**: The inquiry is getting nowhere. We'll have to start again from scratch.

Yeux

Loins des yeux, loin de coeur
Out of sight, out of mind.

Il ne faut pas avoir les yeux
plus grands que le ventre.
You shouldn't bite off more
than you can chew.

Test Yourself!

PETITES REVISIONS 6
What is the missing word?

(Answers on page 128)

1. Des vacances hors des - - - - battus. (off the beaten track)
2. Sur la scène un jeune homme était assis en - - - - - -. (to sit cross-legged)
3. Il est parti sans - - - ni trompette. (to leave unobtrusively)
4. Le bon vieux - - - - - -. (the good old days)
5. Il est à - - - et à toi avec beaucoup de ses clients. (to be on familiar terms)
6. On nous l'a répété sur tous les - - - - -. (over and over again)
7. Cette fois j'espère joindre l'utile à l'- - - - - .(to mix business with pleasure)
8. Nous l'avons fait contre vents et - - - - -. (against all the odds)
9. Le chien courait - - - - à terre. (to run flat out)
10. Je le connais mieux que vous. Il se - - - dans un verre d'eau. (to get into a state over small problems)
11. Un numéro - - - - - -. (freephone number)
12. C'est un voeu - - - - -. (wishful thinking)
13. La voie est - - - - -. (the coast is clear)
14. Vouloir c'est - - - - -. (where there's a will there's a way)
15. Nous avons dû repartir à - - - -. (to start from scratch)

Answers

Petites Révisions 1

1. ailes
2. prison
3. ange
4. angles
5. argent
6. balle
7. barrière/
   barricade
8. bâtons
9. beau
10. ongles
11. panse
12. croisés
13. case
14. bois
15. os

Petites Révisions 2

1. chaises
2. chat
3. écoliers
4. quatre
5. coeur
6. conseil
7. couleur
8. couteaux
9. coutume
10. date
11. deux
12. plaise
13. vie
14. saints
15. éléphant

Petites Révisions 3

1. épée
2. rencontrent
3. étoile
4. feu
5. comble
6. coeur
7. fusil
8. facile
9. gant
10. gare
11. glace/marbre
12. grand
13. guichets/
    bureaux
14. toutes
15. joue/travaille

Petites Révisions 4

1. comptés
2. chantent
3. loup
4. malheur
5. marteau
6. mot
7. noeud
8. noire
9. oeuf
10. ombre
11. os
12. paroisse
13. cent
14. peau
15. pied

Petites Révisions 5

1. coups
2. dorer
3. avaler
4. poche
5. poire
6. pomme
7. campent/
   restent
8. basse
9. quoi
10. matière
11. carrosse
12. rues
13. sac
14. saint
15. salut

Petites Révisions 6

1. sentiers
2. tailleur
3. tambour
4. temps
5. tu
6. tons
7. agréable
8. marées
9. ventre
10. noie
11. vert
12. pieux
13. libre
14. pouvoir
15. zéro